HIGH VOICE

Songs through the Centuries

41 VOCAL REPERTOIRE PIECES FROM THE 17TH THROUGH THE 20TH CENTURIES

Compiled and Edited by Bernard Taylor

Accompaniment tapes
with texts of non-English songs spoken by native speakers
are available through:
Pocket Coach Publications
19850 Lake Chabot Road
Castro Valley, CA 94546
Telephone (510) 886-8875; Fax (510) 886-0244

CARL FISCHER®
62 Cooper Square, New York, NY 10003

ATF110

ISBN 0-8258-0388-8

Foreword

In preparing this volume of songs, extensive research and care have been taken to find material that is now or should be part of the basic vocal repertoire.

The songs selected for inclusion cover a wide range of levels from easy to moderately difficult, making the collection usable by the beginning performer as well as the advanced artist-singer.

Another consideration in creating this collection was that it should be suitable for use by individual singers, group classes and by master-class instructors.

In editing these songs the following symbols have been used to indicate suggested breathing points:

    1). The mark ❯ is used to indicate where the phrase begins and ends.
    2). The sign (❯) is used to indicate an emergency place to breathe.
    3). The sign o is used to indicate where a rest should be observed, but no breath be taken.

For greater accessibility to all singers, this comprehensive collection has been made available for both high (ATF 110) and low (ATF111) voices.

Bernard U. Taylor

Table of Contents

Drink to Me Only with Thine Eyes

Ben Jonson
(1573-1637)

Old English Air

ATF110

soul __ doth rise, Doth ask a drink __ di - vine; _____

But might I of Love's nec - tar sip __ I would __ not change for

thine. _____ I sent thee late a

ro - sy wreath, __ Not so __ much hon - 'ring thee _____

As giv-ing it a hope_ that there_ It could_ not with - er'd

be; _____ But thou_ there -on didst on - ly breathe, And

sent'st it back_ to me,_____ Since when it grows, and smells,_ I swear,_ Not

of _ it - self, but thee. _____

pp

dim. e rit.

pp

Have You Seen But the Whyte Lillie Grow

Ben Jonson
(1573-1637)

Anonymous, 1614

ev - er; Or have smelt of the bud of the bryer, Or the nard in the fire, Or have

tast - ed the bag of the bee. Oh so whyte, Oh so soft, Oh so

sweet, so sweet,_____ so sweet is shee! Oh so whyte, Oh so

soft, Oh so sweet, so sweet,_____ so sweet is shee!

The Lass with a Delicate Air

MICHAEL ARNE
(1741-1786)

1. Young Mol - ly who __ liv'd at the foot __ of __ the __ hill, Whose fame __ ev - 'ry __ vir - gin with en - vy doth fill, Of beau - ty __ is __ bless'd with __ so __ am - ple a __ share, __ Men

ev'n - ing last __ May as I trav - ers'd the __ grove, In thought - less __ re - tire - ment not dream - ing of love, I chanc'd to __ es - py the __ gay - nymph, I __ de - clare, __ And

call her — the — lass with the del - i - cate air, with the
real - ly — she — had a most del - i - cate air, a most

del - - - - - i - cate air, — Men
del - - - - - i - cate air, — And

call — her — the — lass — with — the — del - i - cate air.
real - ly — she — had — a — most — del - i - cate air.

*1. One

* This verse may be omitted.

ATF110

3. By a mur - mur - ing ___ brook on a green ___ mos - sy ___ bed, A chap - let ___ com - pos - ing, the fair - one was laid; Sur - pris'd and ___ trans - port - ed ___ I ___ could not for - bear ___ With rap - ture ___ to ___ gaze on her del - i - cate air, on her del -

con grazia (daintily)

- - i - cate air,__ with rap - ture to__ gaze__ on__ her__

colla voce

del - i - cate__ air.

4. A thou - sand times__ o'er I've re - peat - ed__ my__ suit, But

still__ the tor - men - tor af - fects__ to be mute! Then tell me,__ ye__

swains who have con-quer'd the fair, How to win the dear

lass with the del-i-cate air, with the del-

con grazia (daintily)

-i-cate air, How to win the dear

lass with the del-i-cate air.

rit.

ten. **p** *a tempo*

Air from "Comus"

(Preach not me your musty rules)

John Milton
(1608-1674)

THOMAS AUGUSTINE ARNE
(1710-1778)

Preach not me ____ your mus - ty rules, Ye drones that mould ____ in

i - dle cell, _____ The heart is wis - er than___ the schools, The sen - ses al - ways rea - son well. If short my span I less___ can spare to pass a sin - gle

Under the Greenwood Tree

from *As You Like It*, Act II, Scene 5

William Shakespeare
(1564-1616)

THOMAS AUGUSTINE ARNE
(1710-1778)

Here shall he see___ no en-e-my, but win-ter and rough

weath - er. Here shall he see___ no en-e-my, but win-ter and rough

weath- er. Here shall he see___ no en-e-my, but win - ter, But

win - ter and rough weath - er, rough weath -er, But win - ter and rough weath -er.

Un - der the Green - wood Tree, who

loves __ to live with me, And tune __ his mer - ry note un - to the

sweet bird's throat, And tune his mer - ry note un - to __ the

sweet bird's throat, Come hith - er, hith - er, hith - er,

hith - er, come hith - er, come hith - er, come hith - er, come hith - er, come

hith - er, come hith - er, come hith - er.

When Love is Kind

Thomas Moore
(1779-1852)

Old Melody

When love is kind,_____ cheer - ful and free,_____ Love's sure to

find_____ wel - come from me. But when love brings_____

heart - ache and pang,_____ Tears and such things,_____ Love may go

hang.

scherzando

rit.

p *dolce*

If love can sigh _____ for one a - lone, _____ Well pleas'd am

p *dolce*

con grazia

I _____ to be that one, But should I see _____

colla voce

f animandosi

f

Love giv'n to rove _____ To two or three, _____ then good - bye,

f

f

Long, Long Ago

Thomas Haynes Bayley

THOMAS HAYNES BAYLEY
(1797-1839)

1. Tell me the tales that to me were so dear,
2. Do you re - mem - ber the path where we met,
3. Though by your kind - ness my fond hopes were raised,

Long, long a - go, long, long a - go: Sing me the songs I de -
Long, long a - go, long, long a - go? Ah! yes, you told me you
Long, long a - go, long, long a - go; You, by more el - o - quent

29

light - ed to hear, Long, long a - go, long a - go.
ne'er would for - get, Long, long a - go, long a - go.
lips have been praised, Long, long a - go, long a - go.

Now_ you are come, all my grief_ is re - mov'd, Let_ me for - get that so
When_ to all o - thers my smile_ you pre - ferr'd, Love,_ when you spoke, gave a
But_ by long ab - sence your truth_ has been tried, Still_ to your ac - cents I

long_ you have rov'd, Let me be - lieve that you love as you lov'd
charm_ to each word, Still my heart trea - sures the prais - es I heard
lis - ten with pride, Blest as I was when I sat at your side

rit.

Long , long a - go, long a - go.
Long, long a - go, long a - go.
Long, long a - go, long a - go.

rit.

A Pastorale
(Flocks Are Sporting)

Eighteenth Century Air

HENRY CAREY
(1690-1743)

Flocks are sport - ing, doves are court - ing, Warb - ling
Flocks are bleat - ing, rocks re - peat - ing, Val - leys

lin - nets sweet - ly sing, Ah! ——————
e - cho back the sound,

ATF110

Lo! Here the Gentle Lark

from *Venus and Adonis*

William Shakespeare
(1564-1616)

HENRY ROWLEY BISHOP
(1786-1855)

from whose sil - ver breast The sun _____ a -

ris - eth in true ma - jes - ty, the

sun _____ a - ris - eth in true _____

cresc. *f* *p* *f*

Shepherd! Thy Demeanour Vary

Eighteenth Century Air

THOMAS BROWN
18th Century

Shep - herd! thy de - mean - our va - ry, Dance__ and sing,__ be

light_____ and air - y, Dance_____

you __ must __ woo __ As __ a lov - - er brave and true.

Hums and ha's, dull looks and sigh - ing,

And such sim - ple meth - ods try - ing, Nev - er will this

heart _____ sub-due, _____ I __ must _ catch __ the flame __ from you, Must

It Was a Lover and His Lass
from *As You Like It,* Act V, Scene 3

William Shakespeare
(1564-1616)

THOMAS MORLEY
(1557-1603)

spring - time, the on - ly pret - ty ring time, When birds do sing, hey ding-a-ding-a-ding, hey

ding-a-ding-a-ding, hey ding-a-ding-a-ding, hey ding-a-ding-a-ding, Sweet lov - ers love the spring, in spring - time.

In spring - time, the on - ly pret - ty ring time, When birds do sing, hey

ding-a-ding-a-ding, hey ding-a-ding-a-ding, hey ding-a-ding-a-ding, Sweet lov - ers love the spring.

Passing By

Anonymous poem from Thomas Ford's
Musicke of Sundrie Kindes, 1607

EDWARD C. PURCELL
(1653-?1717)

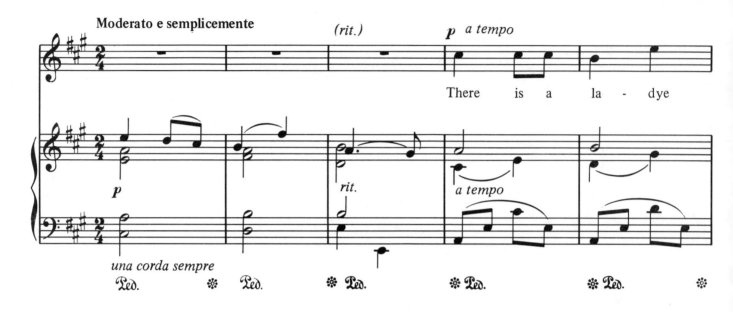

yet I love her till I die.

Her ges - tures, mo - tions and her smile, Her wit, her voice my heart ___ be - guile, Be - guile ___ my heart, I know not why, And yet I

My Lovely Celia

GEORGE MONRO
(1680-1731)

My love - ly _ Ce - lia, heav'n - ly _ fair, As li - lies _ sweet, as soft _ as _ air; No more _ then tor - ment _ me, but _ be _ kind, And with _ thy _ love _ ease my trou - - bled

Non è ver

('Tis Not True)

English text Alice Mattullath

TITO MATTEI, Op. 20, No. 1
(1841-1914)

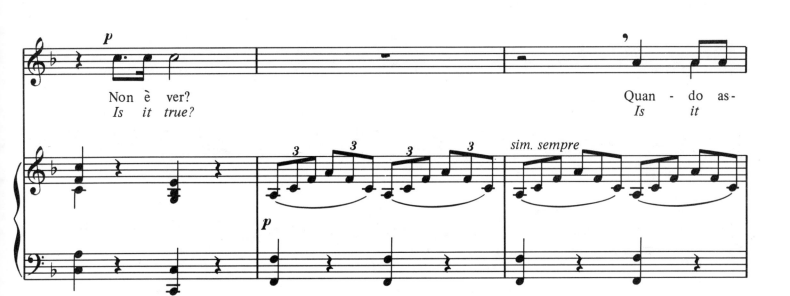

Non è ver?
Is it true?

Quan - do as -
Is it

si - so a te vi - cin,
true, dost thou re - call

Ti par - lai ben mio d'a -
That I gave my heart to

mor, Ti ri - cor - di, an - gel di - vin, Pal - pi -
thee, When in love's first ec - sta - sy At thy

ta - ron i no - stri cor.
feet ___ I laid mine all!

Quan - do as - si - so a te vi - cin,
Is it true, dost thou re - call?

Ti par - lai ben mio d'a -
That my heart I gave to

Tempo I

No, non è ver!
It is not true!

Ah!___ Tu di - ce - sti, ti sov -
Ah!___ All my love for thee was

vien? Per la vi - ta io t'a - me - rò, Ma men -
vain, And thy heart was___ false to me; Ne'er in

ti - sti, in - de - gna, ap-pien, Non fu il cor che tel det -
thee I'll trust a - gain, ne'er re - pose my faith in

58

ATF110

Amarilli, mia bella

GIULIO CACCINI
(1546-1614)

vale. A - pri - mi il pet - to e ve - drai scrit - to in co -

re: A - ma - ril - li, A - ma - ril -

li, A - ma - ril - li è il mio a - mo - re; A - ma -

ril - li_____ è il mio a - mo - re.

Per la gloria d'adorarvi

from the opera *Griselda*

GIOVANNI (Battista) BONONCINI*
(1670-1747)

Per ___ la glo – ria d'a – do – rar – vi vo – glio a –

mar – vi, o lu – ci ca – re; Per ___ la

*N.B. Battista is *not* correct despite the fact that this name appears on some of his compositions. It is simply Giovanni Bononcini.

glo - ria d'a - do - rar - vi vo-glio a - mar - vi, o lu - ci ca - re. A - man-do pe - ne - rò, —— ma sem-pre v'a-me-rò, —— sì, sì —— nel mio —— pe-na - re: A - man-do pe-ne - rò, —— ma sem-pre v'a-me - rò, —— sì,

sì,____ nel mio ____ pe - na - - re, pe - ne - rò, v'a - me - rò,

lu - ci ca - - re, pe - ne - rò, v'a - me - rò, lu - ci ca - -

ro.

Sen - za spe - me di____ di -

let - to va - no af - fet - to è so-spi - ra - - re, Sen - za

spe - me di ___ di - let - to va - no af - fet - to è so-spi -

ra - - re, Ma i vo-stri dol-ci ra - i chi ___ va-gheg-giar può

mai ___ e non, ___ e non ___ v'a-ma - re?

Ma-i vo-stri dol-ci ra-i chi va-gheg-giar può mai e
non, e non v'a-ma-re? Pe-ne-rò, v'a-me-rò, lu-ci ca-
re, Pe-ne-rò, v'a-me-rò, lu-ci ca-re!
deciso
rall.

Vittoria, mio core!

(Victorious My Heart is)

English text by H. Millard

GIAN GIACOMO CARISSIMI
(1605-1674)

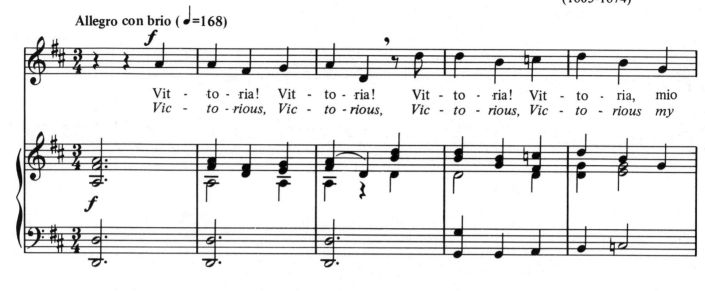

to - ria! Vit - to - ria, mio co - - re! Non la - gri - mar
to - rious, Vic - to - rious, my heart ___ is! And tears are in

più, È sciol - ta ___ d'A - mo - re ___ La ___ vil ser - vi -
vain, For love now ___ has ___ bro - ken ___ its ___ shack - les in

tù, È sciol - - - - - -
twain, For love _____

- - - ta d'A - mo - re La ser - vi - tù.
now has bro - ken its shack - les in twain.

meno mosso, e dolce assai

p

Già l'em-pia a' tuoi dan-ni Fra stuo-lo di sguar-di, Con
The false one is van-quish'd, her glan-ces a-muse me, De-

vez-zi bu-giar-di Di-spo-se gl'in-gan - ni; Le fro-de, gli af-
cep-tion no long-er with arts can con-fuse me! No false-hood or

cresc.

fan-ni Non han-no più lo - co, Del cru-do suo
sor-row op-press me with rig - or, The flame, once so

Tempo I

f

fo-co È spen-to l'ar-do - - re! Vit-to-ria! Vit-
cru-el, has spent all its vig - - or! Vic-to-rious! Vic-

ATF110

to - ria! Vit - to - ria! Vit - to - ria, mio co - - re! Non
to - rious! Vic - to - rious! Vic - to - rious my heart ___ is! And

la - gri - mar più, Non la - gri - mar più, È sciol - ta d'A - mo - re La
tears are in vain, And tears are in vain, For love now has bro - ken its

vil ser - vi - tù, È sciol - - - - ta
shack - les in twain, For love ___

d'A - mo - re La ser - vi - tù!
now has bro - ken its shack les in twain!

to - ria! Vit - to - ria! Vit - to - ria! Vit - to - ria, mio co - re! Non
to - rious, Vic - to - rious, Vic - to - rious, Vic - to - rious my heart__ is! And

la - gri - mar più, Non la - gri - mar più, È sciol - ta d'A -
tears are in vain, And tears are in vain, For love now has

mo - re La vil ser - vi - tù, È sciol - - - -
bro - ken its shack - les in twain, For love_____

- - - - ta d'A - mo - re La ser - vi - tù!
_____ now has bro - ken its shack - les in twain!

Danza, danza, fanciulla gentile

FRANCESCO DURANTE
(1684-1755)

Dan - za,___ dan - za, fan - ciul - la,___ al___ mi - o can -

tar; dan - za,___ dan - za,___ fan - ciul - la gen - ti - le, al

mi - o can - tar. Gi - ra leg -

ge - ra, sot - ti - - - le

al suo - no, al suo - no del

l'on - de_ del_ mar. Sen - ti_il va - go_ ru -

mo - re del l'au - ra_ scher - zo - sa che par - la_ al _

co - re con lan - gui - do___ suon, con_____ lan -

- gui - do _____ suon,   e___ che in -

vi - ta a dan - zar   sen - za   po -

sa,   sen - za   po - sa, che in - vi - ta a dan -

Ave Maria

Sir Walter Scott (1771-1832)
from *The Lady of the Lake*
German text by P. Adam Storck

FRANZ SCHUBERT, Op. 52, No. 6
(1797-1828)

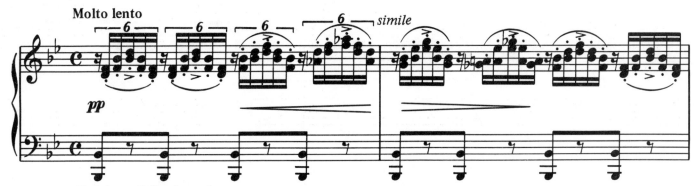

piled, / deckt, / bis,
If __ thy / wird __ weich / O - ra
pro - tec - tion, thy __ pro- / der har - te Fels __ uns / o - ra __ pro no - -

tec - - - - - - - tion hov- er there. / dün - - - - - ken. / bis _____ pec - ca - to - ri - bus
The / Du / nunc

murk - y cav - ern's heav - y air _____ / lä - chelst, Ro - sen-düf - te we - hen / et in ho - ra ____ mor - tis,
Shall / in / in

breathe of balm __ if thou __ hast smiled; / die ser dump - fen Fel - sen-kluft; / ho - ra mor - tis no - strae,
Then / O / in

Maid - en, hear a maid - en's pray - er,
Mut - ter, hör' des kin - des Fle - hen,
ho - ra mor - tis, mor - tis no - strae,
O
O
in

Moth - er, hear a sup - pli - ant child!
Mut - ter, ei - ne Jung - frau ruft!
ho - ra mor - tis no - strae.

p a tempo
a tempo

A - ve Ma - ri -
A - ve Ma - ri -
A - ve Ma - ri -

a!
a!
a!

Plaisir d'amour
(The Joys of Love)

English text by H. Millard

GIOVANNI MARTINI
(1741-1816)

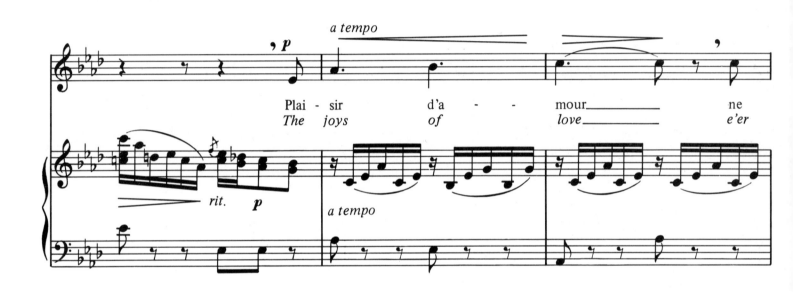

Plai - sir d'a - mour_____ ne
The joys of love_____ e'er

du - re qu'un mo - ment:_____ cha - grin d'a -
swift - ly do__ de - part,_____ Its sor - rows

mour du - re tou - te la vi - - - e.
bit - ter thro'___ a life - time prove.

J'ai tout quit -
I gave up

té pour l'in - gra - te Syl - vi - - - e;___
all ___ for cru - el Syl - via's love,___

el - le me quit - te et prend ___ un au - tre a
Too soon I find an - oth - er owns her

mant.
heart.

Plai -
The

sir   d'a -   mour   ne   du - re   qu'un   mo -
joys   of   love   e'er   swift - ly   do   de -

ment: ___   cha - grin   d'a -   mour du - re   tou - te   la ___
part, ___   Its   sor - rows   bit - ter   thro' ___   a ___

vi -   -   time   e.
life -   time   prove.

"Tant que cet-te eau cou-le-ra dou-ce-
"Long as this brook-let shall soft-ly on-ward

ment____ vers ce ruis-seau qui bor-de la__ prai-ri-e
flow,____ The mead-ow-pass-ing on__ its joy-ous way,____

je t'ai-me-rai," mê ré-pe-tait__ Syl-
Thee I__ will love," ev-er would Syl-via

vi-e. L'eau cou-le en-cor,____ el-
say.____ Still flows__ the stream,____ but

Bist du bei mir

(Abide with Me)

JOHANN SEBASTIAN BACH
(1685-1750)

zum ster - ben __ und zu mei - ner __ Ruh' zum __ Ster-ben und zu mei - ner
The jour - ney __ to that far - off __ land Where __ sor-rows cease and all is

Ruh'! Ach, wie ver - gnügt wär' so mein En - de,
peace. What sweet con - tent To have thee near __ me

es drück - ten __ dei - ne lie ben __ Hän - de mir __ die ge - treu - en Au - gen
Where I __ may __ clasp thine hand __ so __ gen - tle And __ gaze in - to thy faith-ful

zu! Ach wie ver - gnügt wär' so mein
eyes. What sweet con - tent To have thee

En - de, es drück - ten __ dei - ne lie - ben __ Hän - de mir __
near me Where I __ may clasp thine hand __ so gen - tle And __

die ge - treu - en Au - gen zu! Bist du __ bei __ mir,
gaze in - to thy faith - ful eyes. A - bide __ with __ me,

geh' ich mit Freu - den zum Ster - ben __ und zu mei - ner
Then will I fear not The jour - ney __ to that far - off __

Ruh', zum _____ Ster - ben und zu mei - ner Ruh'!
land Where _____ sor - rows cease and all is peace.

Care Selve

from the opera *Atalanta*

GEORGE FRIDERIC HANDEL
(1685-1759)

Ca - - - re Sel - ve,
Come, my be - lov - ed!

Ca - re, ca - re Sel - ve,
Through the syl - van gloom I

om - bre be - a - te, Ven -
wan - der day and night, Oft

string.

ATF110

Ridente la Calma

(Canzonetta, K. 210A)

WOLFGANG AMADEUS MOZART, K.152
(1756-1791)

Ri - den - te la cal - ma nell'- al - ma_ si_

de - sti, nell'- al - ma_ si _ de-sti; ne

re - sti un se - gno di sde - gn e ti - mor. Ri - den - te la

cal - ma nell'-al - ma si de - sti; ne re - sti piu se - gno di

sde - gno e ti - mor, ne re - sti più se - gno di sde - gno e ti -

mor, di sde - gno e ti - mor. Tu

vie - ni frat - tan - to a strin - ger mio be - ne le dol - ci __ ca -

ATF110

te - ne si gra - te al mio cor,_____ si gra - te al mio

cor,_____ si gra - te al mio cor. Ri - den - te la

cal - ma nell' - al - ma si_ de - sti, nell' - al - ma_ si_ de - sti;

ne re - sti un se - gno di sde - gno e ti -

mor. Ri - den - te la cal - ma nell'- al - ma si de - sti, ne

re - sti più se - gno di sde - gno e ti - mor, ne

re - sti più se - gno di sde - gno e ti - mor, di

sde - gno e ti - mor.

Wiegenlied
(Lullaby)

Friedrich Wilhelm Gotter
English text Alice Mattullath

J. BERNHARD FLIES*
(1770- ?)

1. Schla - fe, mein Prinz-chen, es ruh'n   Schäf-chen und Vö - gel - chen
2. Al - les im Schlos-se schon liegt,   Al - les in Schlum-mer ge -
3. Wer ist be-glück - ter, als du?   Nichts als Ver gnü - gen und

1. Sleep lit - tle dar - ling and rest,   Bird-ies have gone to their
2. All are at rest in the house,   Ev - en the lit - tle gray
3. Thine is a life full of joys,   Sweet-meats and plen - ty of

nun,   Gar - ten und Wie - se ver - stummt,   auch nicht ein Bien-chen mehr
wiegt;   re - get kein Mäus-chen sich mehr,   Kel - ler und Kü - che sind
Ruh,   Spiel-werk und zu-cker voll - auf,   und noch Ka - ros-sen im
nest,   Si - lence on mead-ow and lea,   No-where the hum of a
mouse;   Night now her vig - il doth keep,   On - ly a maid finds no
toys,   All that is hap - py and bright,   All that will give thee de -

*For years *Wiegenlied* has been erroneously attributed to W. A. Mozart and was assigned No. 350 in Köchel's catalog.
Max Friedländer discovered the original edition bearing Flies' name as early as 1896. The song has since been relegated
to the Köchel Supplement where full particulars are to be found under Anhang, No. 284F.

Ich liebe dich
(I Love Thee)

Gerdicht von Herrosee
English text by Alice Mattullath

LUDWIG van BEETHOVEN, Grove: Op. 235
(1770-1827)

Andante

Ich lie - be dich, so wie du mich, am A - bend und am Mor - gen, noch_
*I love thee as thou lov - est me, at noon, at eve and mor - row, and_*

war kein Tag, wo du und ich nicht theil - ten un - sre_ Sor - gen;
ev - 'ry day I shared with thee each lit - tle joy_ and_ sor - row;

Auch_ wa - ren sie für dich und mich ge - theilt, leicht zu_ er - tra - gen, du
In_ storm and strife u - nit - ed we, in_ dark and sun - ny_ weath - er; if

trös - te - test im Kum - mer mich, ich_ weint' in dei - ne Kla - gen, in dei - ne
fate to eith - er cru - el be, we'd_ bear the cross to - geth - er, the cross to -

Still wie die Nacht

(Calm as the Night)

English text by Alice Mattullath

CARL BOHM, Op. 326, No. 27
(1844-1920)

Quietly, but not too slow

Still wie die Nacht, tief wie das
Still as the night, deep as the

Meer, _____ soll dei - ne Lie - be sein! _____
sea, _____ For me thy love_____ should be! _____

Die Lotosblume
(The Lotus Flower)

Heinrich Heine (1797-1886)
English text by Alice Mattullath

ROBERT SCHUMANN, Op. 25, No. 7
(1810-1856)

Die Lo - tos - blu - me äng - stigt
The Lo - tos flow-er is droop - ing,

sich vor der Son - ne Pracht,
fear-ing the sun's warm ray;

und mit ge - senk - tem Haup - te,
fold-ing her dew - y pe - tals, she

er -
she

war - tet sie träu - mend die Nacht.
longs for the close of day.

Der Mond der ist ihr Buh - le,
She loves the sil - ver moon - light that

er
that

Edward

Old Scottish Ballad
German text *Stimmen der Völker*
by Johann Gottfried Herder (1744-1803)

CARL LOEWE, Op. 1, No. 1
(1796-1869)

Dein Schwert wie ist's von Blut so roth, Ed - ward,
Why does your brand sae drop wi' bluid, *Ed - ward,*

Ed - ward! dein Schwert wie ist's von Blut so roth, und
Ed - ward! Why does your brand sae drop wi' bluid, *And*

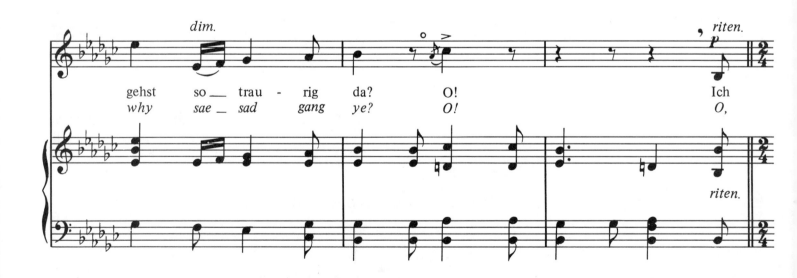

gehst so trau - rig da? O! Ich
why sae sad gang ye? *O!* *O,*

dein Ross war alt und hast's nicht noth, dich drückt ein an - d'rer
Your steed was auld, ye hae gat mair, Some oth - er dule ye

Schmerz. O! Ich hab' ge-schla-gen mei-nen
drie, O! O I hae kill-ed my

Va - ter todt, Mut - ter, Mut - ter! ich
fa - ther dear, Mith - er, Mith - er! O

hab' ge-schla-gen mei-nen Va - ter todt, und das,
I hae kill-ed my fa - ther dear, A - las,

das   quält mein Herz!   O!_____
wae,   wae is   me,   O!_____

decresc.

morendo

Und was wirst   du   nun   an   dir
What pen - ance will ye   drie for

thun?   Ed - ward,   Ed - ward!   und was wirst du   nun   an   dir
that?   Ed - ward,   Ed - ward!   What pen-ance will ye   drie   for_____

wan-dern ü-ber's Meer! O!
I'll fare o'er the sea, O!

Und was soll wer-den dein Hof und Hall'? Ed-ward, Ed-ward!
And what will ye do wi' your towers and ha'? Ed-ward, Ed-ward!

und was soll wer-den dein Hof und Hall'? so herr-lich sonst, so
And what will ye do wi' your towers and ha'? That were sae fair to

schön. O! Ach im-mer
see, O! I'll let them

Und was soll wer-den aus Weib und Kind, wenn du gehst ü-ber's
And what will ye leave to your bairns and wife, When ye gang o'er the

Meer? O! Die Welt ist
sea? O! The warld is

a tempo

gross, lass'_ sie_ bett-eln drin, Mut-ter! Mut-ter! Die Welt ist gross,_
room, let_ them_ beg thro' life, Mith-er, Mith-er! The warld is room,_

a tempo

_____ lass'_ sie_ bet-teln drin, ich, ich seh' sie
_____ let_ them_ beg thro' life, Them, them nae mair
(non arpegg.)

ff

ff

p

Höl - - le soll auf euch ruh'n,
hell *frae* *me* *shall* *ye* *bear,*

Mut - ter, Mut - ter!
Mith - *er,* *Mith* - *er!*

Der Fluch der Höl - - le soll
The *curse* *of* *hell* *frae*

auf euch ruh'n denn ihr, ihr rie-thet's mir! O!
me *shall* *ye* *bear,* *'Twas* *you* *sae* *coun-selled me,* *O!*

con ped.

ff

Ich atmet' einen linden Duft

Friedrich Rückert
(1788-1866)

GUSTAV MAHLER
(1860-1911)

lin - de! Ich at - me leis____

____ im Duft ___ der Lin - de der

Lie - - be lin - den Duft.

An die Musik

Franz von Schober

FRANZ SCHUBERT, Op. 88, No. 4
(1810-1856)

bess' - re Welt ent - ruckt, in ei - ne bess' - re Welt ___ ent -

rückt.

Oft hat ein Seuf - zer,

dei - ner Harf ___ ent - flos - sen, ein sü - sser

hei - li - ger Ac - cord_ von_ dir, den Him - mel

bess' - rer Zei - ten mir_ er_ schloss - en; du hol - de Kunst,_ ich

dan - ke dir da - fur, du hol - de Kunst_ ich dan - ke dir.

Widmung
(Dedication)

Friedrich Rückert (1788-1866)
English text by Sigmund Spaeth

ROBERT SCHUMANN, Op. 25, No. 1
(1810-1856)

130

ATF110

Schmerz, du mei-ne welt, ___ in der ich le- be, mein Him- mel
woe! *All of my world, ___ my life un-end- ing, My* — en

du, ___ dar- ein ich schwe be, mein gu- ter Geist, mein bess,- res
too, ___ this earth tran- scend- ing, My bet- ter self I find ___ in

Ich!
thee!

Il pleure dans mon coeur

(It Cries In My Heart)

No. 2 from *Ariettes oubliées*

Paul Verlaine (1844-1896)
English text by Alice Mattullath

ACHILLE CLAUDE DEBUSSY
(1862-1918)

Quelle est cet- te lan - gueur   Qui pé -
Why this wea - ry dull pain   Creep - ing

nè - - tre mon coeur? _____
o'er _____ me a - gain?

O bruit doux de la ___ plui - e   Par terre et sur les
Rain sooth - ing sound is mak - ing ___   On the stones of the

toits! _____
street. _____

Pour   un   coeur   qui   s'en -
To   *a*   *heart*   *that*   *is*

nui   -   e   O   le   chant
ach   -   *ing*   *Sings*   *the*   *rain,*

de   la   pluie!   Il
low   *and*   *sweet!*   *I*

son.

grieve.

accel. poco a poco al Tempo I

Tempo I

C'est bien la pi - re pei -
To un - known grief a - wak - ing,

ne De ne sa - voir pour - quoi, Sans a -
That naught can e'er re - lieve, Not with

mour et sans hai - ne,
hate or love ach - ing,

ATF110

Mon coeur a tant de pei - - - - ne!
My heart is nigh to break - - - - ing!

per - den - do - si e poco rit.

Mandoline

Paul Verlaine (1844-1896)
English text by Alice Mattullath

ACHILLE CLAUDE DEBUSSY
(1862-1918)

ses. _____ C'est Tir - cis et c'est _ A - min - - te,
ing. _____ Thyr – sis fair A - min - ta woo - - ing,

Et C'est l'é - ter - nel Cli - tan - - - dre, Et c'est Da - mis qui
And that Cli - tan - der so bor - - - ing, Da - mon the cru - el

pour main - te cru - el - le fait _ maint vers tend - dre. _____
maid - ens pur - su - ing in vers - es a - dor - ing. _____

Leurs cour - tes ves - tes de soie, Leurs lon - gues ro - bes à _____
Their dou - blets silk - en and bright, Their gowns be - ruf - fled are _____

queu - es, Leur é - lé - gan - ce, Leur joi - e Et leurs mol - les
trail - ing, *Their court-ly style,* *their de - light,* *Their* *shad - ows, — the*

om - bres __ bleu - es, Tour - bil - lon - nent dans __ l'ex-ta - se
pic - ture __ veil - ing, *Whirl in rap - ture toned __ dis-creet-ly*

D'u - ne lu - ne rose __ et gri - se, Et la man-do - li - ne ja - se
Rose-gray moon-beams o'er __ them stray-ing. *The man-do - lin tink - les sweet - ly,*

par - mi les fris - sons de bri - - se. La,
Fit - ful-ly zeph - yrs are play - - ing *La,*

Cantique de Noël
(O Holy Night)

ADOLPHE ADAM
(1803-1856)

Andante maestoso

Mi-nuit, ___ Chré - tien, ___ c'est l'heu-re so - len-
O ho - ly night,___ the stars are bright-ly

nel - le Où l' Hom-me Dieu de -scen-dit jus-qu'à nous,
shin - ing, It is the night of the dear Sav-iour's birth.

Pour ef - fa - cer ___ la ta-che ori - gi - nel - le Et de son
Long lay the world ___ in sin and er - ror pin - ing Till he ap-

come prima

ATF110

den - te Nous gui - de tous au ber - ceau de l'en - fant,
beam - ing, with glow - ing hearts by His cra - dle stand.

Comme au - tre - fois une é - toi - le bril - lan - te y con - dui -
So led by light of a star sweet - ly gleam - ing, Here came the

sit les chefs—— de l'o - ri - ent.———— Le Roi des Rois naît
wise— men from the O - rient land.———— The King of Kings lay

dans une hum - ble crê - che Puis - sants du jour, fiers de vo - tre gran - deur,
thus in low - ly man - ger, In all our tri - als born to be our friend.

teur.
bend.

a tempo

marcato

Lé Ré - demp -
Tru - ly He

teur a bri - sé toute en - tra - ve, La terre est li - bre et le ciel est ou -
taught us to love one an - oth - er, His law is love and His gos - pel is

vert.
peace.

Il voit un frè - re où n'é - tait qu'un es -
Chains shall He break, for the slave is our

150

How Do I Love Thee?

Elizabeth B. Browning
(1806-1861)
Adapted by Norman Dello Joio

NORMAN DELLO JOIO
(1913-   )

Just - Spring

e.e. cummings*
(1894-1962)

JOHN DUKE
(1899-   )

in   just - spring _____   when   the

Copyright © 1954 by Carl Fischer, Inc., New York
62 Cooper Square, New York, NY 10003
International Copyright Secured.
All rights reserved including performing rights.
Printed in the U.S.A.

ATF110

156

ATF110

the queer old ba - loon - man whis-tles

far _____ and wee

and bet-ty-and - is - bel come danc - ing from hop-scotch and

jump - rope   and   it's   spring _____

and the goat - foot - ed ba - loon - man

whis - tles   far _____ and   wee _____

There is a Lady Sweet and Kind

Anonymous Elizabethan

NORMAN DELLO JOIO
(1913-   )

There is a la-dy sweet and kind,____ Was nev-er face so pleased my mind;____

I did but see her, see her pass-ing by, __ And yet I love her till I die.

Her ges-ture,— her mo-tion,— and her smile,— Her wit, her voice — my heart be - guile,— Be-guile my heart, I know not why,— And yet I love her till I die.

There is a la - dy sweet and kind,_____ Was nev-er face so pleased my

mind;_____ If she should change the earth, should change the earth or sky,

Yet will I love her till I die, Yet will I love her till I

die.__

Spring Day

John Egilsrud

EDWIN McARTHUR
(1907-   )

Lento (majestic)

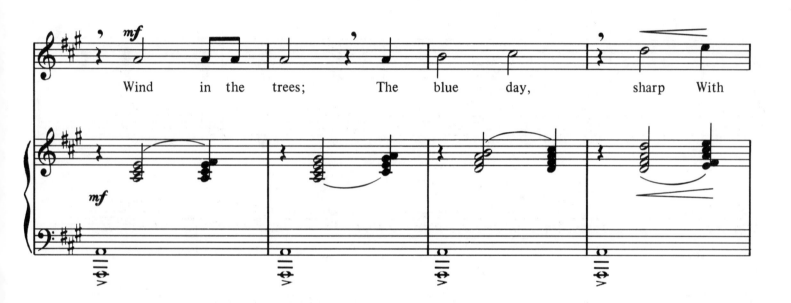

Wind in the trees; The blue day, sharp With

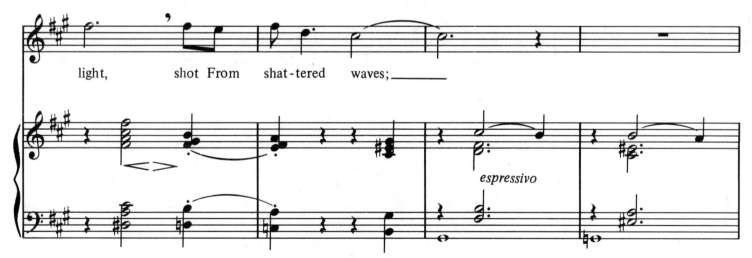

light, shot From shat-tered waves;

espressivo

High, swell-ing clouds Blown sea-ward and west In-to the sky.

Once more the full lung, The flush, And the joy of the

heart Sing-ing loud Through the spa-cious halls Of the

day.

Come Where My Love Lies Dreaming

STEPHEN C. FOSTER
(1826-1864)
Arranged by William Dressler

Moderato

Come where my love lies dream - ing, Dream-ing the hap-py hours a - way, In

vis-ions bright re-deem - ing The fleet-ing joys of day;

rit. *a tempo*

Dream - ing the hap-py hours, Dream-ing the hap-py hours a - way, ___

Come where my love lies dream - ing, is sweet-ly dream -ing the hap-py hours a -way.

Come where my love lies dream - ing, is sweet-ly dream-ing, Her beau-ty beam - ing;

Come where my love lies dream - ing, is sweet-ly dream -ing the hap-py hours a - way.

Come with a lute, come with a lay, My own love is sweet-ly dream-ing, Her beau-ty beam-ing;

Come where my love lies dream - ing, is sweet - ly dream-ing the hap-py hours a - way.

Soft is her slum - ber, Thoughts bright and free Dance thro' her dreams Like

gush -ing mel - o - dy, Light is her young heart, Light may it be!

ATF110

Come where my love lies dream - ing. Dream - ing the hap - py hours,

Dream - ing the hap - py hours a - way, _____ Come where my love lies

dream - ing, is sweet - ly dream - ing the hap - py hours a - way.

Come where my love lies dream - ing, is sweet - ly ing, Her beau - ty beam - ing;

Old Folks at Home
(Way Down upon the Swannee River)

STEPHEN C. FOSTER
(1826-1864)

Moderato espressivo

Way down up-on the Swa-nee riv-er Far, far a - way,
All 'round the lit-tle farm I wan-der'd When I was young,
One lit-tle hut a-mong the bush-es, One that I love,

There's where my heart is turn-ing ev-er, There's where the old folks stay.
Then man-y hap-py days I squand-er'd, Man-y the songs I sung.
Still sad-ly to my mem-'ry rush-es, No mat-ter where I rove.

All up and down the whole cre-a-tion, Sad-ly I roam,
When I was play-ing with my broth-er Hap-py was I,
When will I see the bees a-hum-ming, All 'round the comb?

Still long-ing for the old plan-ta-tion, And for the old folks at home
Oh! take me to my kind old moth-er, There let me live and die.
When will I hear the ban-jo tum-ming, Down in my good old home?

REFRAIN

All the world is sad and drear-y Ev-'ry where I roam.

Oh! broth-ers, how my heart grows wear-y, Far from the old folks at home.

Jeanie with the Light Brown Hair

STEPHEN C. FOSTER
(1826-1864)

Moderato

mp ... *mf*

I dream of Jean-ie with the light brown hair, Borne, like a va-por,

on the sum-mer air; I see her trip-ping where the bright streams play,

cresc. Hap-py as the dai-sies that dance on her way. *f* Man-y were the wild notes her

merry voice would pour, Many were the blithe birds that warbled them o'er. Oh! I

dream of Jeanie with the light brown hair, Floating, like a vapor, on the

soft summer air. I long for Jeanie with the

gay dawn smile, Radiant with gladness, warm with winning guile; I

ATF110

About Bernard Taylor

A native of Olean, New York, Bernard Taylor has had a very active career in music. At an early age he began the study of violin and continued this study until his voice changed. From that time on he has devoted his entire career to singing and the teaching of singing.

Mr. Taylor's main studies were at the University of Pennsylvania and Teachers College at Columbia University. His first post as a teacher of singing was at Texas Christian University in Fort Worth, Texas, where he was also conductor of the Men's Glee Club. After his four years at TCU, he organized and became the first director and president of the Fort Worth Conservatory of Music. Under Taylor's leadership the conservatory gained wide recognition throughout the Southwest.

In 1929, Mr. Taylor returned to New York City where he has resided ever since. Soon after his return, he taught for two summer sessions at Teachers College, Columbia University, and in 1932 he accepted a post at the Juilliard School of Music — a position he held for over 22 years. In 1941, he became one of the founders of the National Association of Teachers of Singing and in 1953 was elected president of this association. In 1944 he was elected President of the New York Singing Teachers Association. Since leaving the Juilliard School, Mr. Taylor has continued teaching through his private studio in New York City.

During his many years as a teacher of singing, Mr. Taylor has taught numerous successful singers in the recital, oratorio and operatic fields. He first introduced group voice for schools, colleges and universities in the 1930's and has conducted over the years innumerable master classes throughout the country. He is well known for his many published vocal albums, including *Contemporary American Songs; Italian, French and German Classic Songs*; and the Carl Fischer publications: *Songs in English* (High voice: O4791—Low voice: O4792) and *Contemporary Songs in English* (High voice: O3819—Low voice: O3820)—all of which are used extensively in schools and colleges today.